Book Two: "Silly" Puppy Series

Why does POOKIE love her Terrier Life?

Lucinda Sue Crosby & Laura Dobbins

Illustrated by Tanja Tadic

LuckyCinda Publishing

USA

Why Does Pookie Love Her Terrier Life?

www.luckycinda.com

FIRST EDITION

Printed in the USA

Library of Congress Control Number: 2017930890

LuckyCinda - www.luckycinda.com

January 11, 2017

ISBN: 978-0-9960898-7-6

Cover and book design by Laura Dobbins
Illustrations by Tanja Tadic: http://bit.ly/1erISda

Dedication:

To all the dogs we've loved before …

Why does POOKIE Love Her Terrier Life?

For Ages 4 to 8 years old

Book Two: "Silly" Puppy Series

Pookie is a rescued dog
as cute as cute can be
who was joyfully adopted by
our loving family

Now she lives
The Terrier Life
chock full of fun and food.
At times she acts just like a brat
but mostly she's quite good!

Every morning, first things first,
we clip her to a leash.
She prances and she sniffs the air
as we walk down the street.

A block or two away from home
she meets friends at the park
She'll wag her tail and tear around
and bark and bark and bark.

And oh how Pookie
loves to eat;
her food is what she craves.
She'll lick her chops
and "dinner dance" –
it's how she celebrates!

Every time she gets a bath
she's washed in pink shampoo.
The bubbles on her shiny nose
Can make her sneeze "achoo."

Pookie's such a tidbit dog
she's small enough to swim
across my mother's
kitchen sink
Oh! There she goes again!

In all her favorite
napping nooks
you'll find a comfy bed.
Each has a puppy
pillow where
a dog can rest her head.

Pookie has a doctor friend
like you and you and me.
She gets a check-up,
then her shots
and then she gets a treat.

When she jumps into the car,
and settles in her place,
we make sure her
seatbelt's on
because it keeps her safe.

Among her tiny, furry toys
are some that yip and squeak.
She tosses them into
the air and rubs them
with her cheek.

When it's time to go to sleep
she likes a larger bed
and snuggles up beside me or
my best sleep-over friend.

As you can see,
our special girl
is doing awfully well.
She's like a little Princess doll
with four paws and a tail.

She's brought us
so much happiness;
she's taught us to be kind;
she's helped us be responsible
and made our patience shine.

We hope you have
some pretty pets
to share your love and home
If not, maybe you'll
rescue one
for a joy you've never known!

THE

END ...

About the Authors

Lucinda Sue Crosby was selected as one of "50 Authors You Should be Reading" in 2011 by *AuthorsFirst* - an online media outlet. She is also an award-winning author, prize winning journalist and environmentalist, Nashville songwriter, commissioned poet, professional athlete and former Hollywood actress. This is Crosby's ninth published book and her third children's story. You can find all of Crosby's books at Amazon.

Crosby is also the proud owner of a rescue dog, the "Silly" Terrier, Pookie.

Laura Dobbins is an award-winning journalist and page designer. She is the co-author of the Global Ebook First Place Winner for Book Marketing: *Sell more Ebooks, how to increase sales and Amazon rankings using Kindle Direct Publishing*. She is also founder of *Kindle Book Promos* - a site dedicated to author features and Kindle book promotions.

Visit http://kindlebookpromos.luckycinda.com for free and paid promos for authors.

Meet Pookie

Pookie is a unique and special dog and I am proud to have rescued her.
- Lucinda Sue Crosby

www.ingramcontent.com/pod-product-compliance
Lightning Source LLC
Chambersburg PA
CBHW041547040426
42447CB00002B/85